◆

Thereafter, yes
call the sea
a poet

mpT
MODERN POETRY
IN TRANSLATION
The best of world poetry

No. 2 2023

© *Modern Poetry in Translation* 2023 and contributors

ISSN (print) 0969-3572
ISSN (online) 2052-3017
ISBN (print) 978-1-910485-36-1

Editor: Khairani Barokka
Managing Editor: Sarah Hesketh
Digital Content Editor: Ed Cottrell
Finance Manager: Deborah de Kock

Creative Apprentice: Chloe Elliott
Design by Brett Evans Biedscheid
Cover art by Daniela 'iella 'Attard
Typesetting by Libanus Press Ltd

Printed and bound in Great Britain by Charlesworth Press, Wakefield
For submissions and subscriptions please visit www.modernpoetryintranslation.com

Modern Poetry in Translation Limited. A Company Limited by Guarantee Registered
in England and Wales, Number 5881603 UK Registered Charity Number 1118223

Cover description: An illustration in black pencil, with a bright red
background. The illustration shows a group of sparrows emerging from an
endless sea, seemingly singing their song, while a traditional Maltese boat
known as a Luzzu emerges from the waves. The sparrow in the foreground
thinks about l-għajn, a motif seen on Luzzu intended to protect fishermen
from harm. The illustration wraps around the back where the scene
continues. In the waves, the sign for 'language' appears in Maltese
Sign Language/Lingwa tas-Sinjali Maltija.

Above left: On the left, the Arts Council England logo curves around in a
circle, next to a black outline of a hand crossing fingers. Underneath both
images, 'LOTTERY FUNDED' is written. In a line on the right, the text
reads, 'Supported using public funding by ARTS COUNCIL ENGLAND'.

Above right: An image of a leaf of paper is coloured in red, emulating a
folded book. Next to it reads the text, *National Book Council*, in black.

MODERN POETRY IN TRANSLATION

Call the Sea a Poet
Focus on Malta

CONTENTS

Focus

Reviews

EDITORIAL

Each group of islands is its own universe. Those that claim islands
will live out our own relationship to the sea, to the wind, to the secret
language of rock formations. For this issue, we are delighted to
present a kaleidoscopic portrait of Maltese poetic voices, translated
from Maltese and/or writing in English (an official language of Malta,
as a former UK colony)—bordered by the sea, speaking to and from it.

The diversity of poetic styles and thematic obsessions here mirror
the manifold influences that have shaped Maltese culture and
linguistics. From Maltese's links to Arabic—as explored in Adrian
Grima's evocative essay in this issue, 'Of Reach and Richness'—to
the Mediterranean wind known as Grigal, that Karina Fiorini writes
of, there are so many ways in which the island's history and natural
environment shape the verse you'll find here.

These Maltese poets write against misogyny, corruption,
discrimination. About the trees of Killarney, Ireland, and of stones
and water. Trials of romance, as in Aaron Aquilina's contribution, or
of parenting, as written and translated by Rita Saliba. How we exist
in natural surroundings, how we may write against injustice, how
we may reflect on our intimate relationships with others and, as in
Miriam Calleja's 'Rebel Dandelion', ourselves. Time and space, sea
and wind, are all imprints on these poetics. Nature's fluidity evincing
the everchanging, evolving nature of linguistic communities.

As Nadia Mifsud writes, in Miriam's Calleja's translation:

> The rainshower stops
> and this city suddenly looks changed.

As Omar Seguna writes, translated by Alfred Palma:

> Now that
> the sea's begun to ebb and flow,
> we can walk on along the shore,

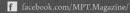

There will always be change to notice, to create, to look forward to. There will always be poets writing from Malta, ever-evolving, a part of its waters.

Elsewhere in this issue are outstanding works in verse in memoriam—see Mohammad-Ali Sepanlou's 'Mosaddegh', translated by Siavash Saadlou, and Adriana Díaz Enciso's translation of the late David Huerta, 'Behold Silence'—in illness, in the face of climate change, and many with an everpresent spiritual in so many shifting guises.

In both the Focus and general section of this issue, there are poems that give us such bodily intimacy, as in Aya Nabih's verse, as translated by Sara Elkamel:

> A nausea stained with the suspicion of absence takes me
> by surprise as I wait for the elevator to come down, and
> permeates my soul on the ride up.

Intimate too are the political insights of Meena Kandasamy, interviewed by Sana Goyal, on the poetics of translating poetry from Tamil, and 'resisting internal colonialism'. Vital perspectives are also found here in incisive reviews on Bengali, Sudanese, and Assamese poetry in English translation, by Adrija Ghosh, Mayada Ibrahim, and Amlanjyoti Goswami respectively.

Opposite: In black and white, various photographs of various former MPT contributors in three rows of six. Below are the MPT logo and motto, 'The best of world poetry', and a quote from John Berger, saying 'ANYONE WHO WANTS TO SEE THE WORLD AND SEE IT CHANGED SHOULD JOIN MPT'. Below that is the ACE logo, as well as a line describing MPT, our social media information, website, and subscription info (£23 a year – UK Subscription, £33 – International Subscription).

As ever, we sit with poems, and with writing on poetry, as gifts of insight and tenderness.

I am deeply grateful to have had the opportunity to engage with Maltese poets and poetics in the process of creating this issue; MPT is deeply thankful for support from and collaboration with the National Book Council of Malta, with thanks in particular to Simona Cassano, Jean Paul Borg, and Justine Somerville. We also thank Arts Council England. My great gratitude as ever to brilliant teammates Sarah, Ed, Debbie and Chloe, and to all others who support the creation of our issues—very importantly, including you, the readers. We hope you enjoy these waters, and call the sea a poet.

ALFREDO ESPINO

Translated by Dylan Carpenter from Spanish

Still today, nearly a century after his death, Alfredo Espino remains
one of El Salvador's most essential poets. Known in his native country
as el poeta niño, the boy poet, Espino's portrayals of his youth spent
in Ahuachapán are pastoral, quiet, and painterly. He is above all a
poet of place and landscape: of orange trees and coffee fields, of cattle
and drovers.

'Holy Thursday' is the final poem in *Jicaras Tristes*, Espino's only
collection, published by friends in the wake of his suicide. It
embodies his poetic: a sentimental attitude toward the world of
home and its rituals, inflected with a soft desperation toward
the harsher facts of life.

Holy Thursday

Tonight, the palm grove and the church appear
enveloped in the silver, misty moon,
and our illusions, all of them, are here
departing in procession, one by one.

The church kneels by the kapok tree in bloom.
Below the peaceful moon, the roads disclose
the idea of someone, someone who goes
leaving behind trails of magnesium.

A quiet Holy Thursday. Choruses
of women pray in indecisive light,
and multitudes of candles scintillate
like an impossible river of fireflies.

CHETANA TIRTHAHALLI

Translated by Madhav Ajjampur from Kannada

Good poetry, great poetry even, is no longer restricted to books and literary magazines and private notebooks. It is everywhere: on Instagram, Facebook, Twitter, WhatsApp groups.

I came across this particular poem on Facebook. I did not know Chetana; my meeting was with the poem alone. I remember being immediately struck by its title. The poem did not disappoint. Dexterous, lyrical, and boasting unusual imagery, the poem impressed me with its mystique. Like I often do with Kannada poems that catch my fancy, I set out to translate it. Helped by some clarifications from the poet along the way, I arrived at the translation you see here.

The Water-Seed of the Heart of the Sun

I sit here, sister, having tasted
the evil of acute enchantment;
the warrior, who leaking blood,
dressed me in a peacock-saree
has turned into a stone.
Inside that stone, sister,
my soul's eternally captive.

Can I wait for time on time?
Can the eyes' heat melt stone?
Will this body last till then,
without turning to dust?
I am a beauty-tree, sister,
fallen from a broken waist;
will I ever find love again?

A burning all day long; at night,
no light within the womb;
at the time I take a tired breath,
hope's rainbow shines forth again;
listen, sister,
here's what it's saying:

'The water-seed that'll
melt the warrior set in stone and
get the beauty-tree to bloom
can be found in the heart of the sun.
If you truly are a woman, seize it and come!'

M P PRATHEESH

Translated by K. Satchidanandan from Malayalam

M P Pratheesh at times uses ordinary objects, lines and colours to create visual poems. Even while not using them, he chooses his words carefully and is never loud. His is a quiet kind of poetry that seems to exist like a natural object, a stone, a blade of grass, a quiet little stream in the wilderness. His poems are often like a whisper, delicate and deft in the way they are composed.

A Strand

A strand of
a word
from an unknown
tongue

as if kept gently
by someone
eons ago
inside this stone.

Opposite: An Indian man with short hair and a moustache smiles directly into the camera, wearing an unbuttoned collared shirt.

Rings

long oval rings
that appear and disappear
under the water

on the shore,
stand in the midnight-shade,
and you will see

remote planets, fiery red,
words, paths that
memories cross

DAVID HUERTA

Translated by Adriana Díaz Enciso from Spanish

I chose and translated 'Behold Silence' on the day of David Huerta's passing, as a way to remember him and pay tribute to him, both as a great poet and dear friend. The silence in the poem encompasses memory, the marks left by the accident of living, as well as their dissolution in a vaster silence—time's contradictory substance made of an immanent continuum that holds us all, and impermanence, which claims us. David's poetry is always alert to this conflict, and to the delicate equilibrium needed to find the meaning of human life at its core. David is present in this poem, while revealing the silence left by his absence. I find meaning in the awareness of that wordless emptiness. This poem first appeared in *Canciones de la vida común* (K editores, Mexico, 2008).

Photo: Barry Domínguez

Behold Silence

Behold silence at the back
of memory: a ring of growing water.
Remembrance, wordless, is reflected there.
There—concentrated
folded within itself—the lived life
keeps to white limits.

Behold the pellucid energies
of immanence
and how thought
—in ceaseless reconstruction—
enters vestibules frozen with time
and, with immaterial nearness, touches
their presence; surrounds them, penetrates them,
begins to make them thaw.

Behold this dissolving, these tottering
dimensions, translucent leaves
of vacant phenomena.
Take one more look at silence
mingled with memory,
enamelled with the oil of thought,
and white, white, white, wordless.

AYA NABIH

Translated by Sara Elkamel from Arabic

Aya Nabih's prose poems 'Forms of Nausea' and 'Cancer' appear in
her exceptional debut poetry collection, *Exercises to Develop Insomnia
Skills* (Al Kotob Khan, 2015). Like many of the pieces in *Exercises…*
the poems I've selected here are taut vignettes that conceal just as
much as they reveal—both about the speaker and the world around
her. The speakers in Nabih's poems are almost always women,
often disillusioned, and never quite at home in their material
surroundings. As these two poems will show, Nabih's writing is at
once confessional and withholding, often evading divulgence with
language laced with humor, irony, and hints of surrealism. Nabih is
based in Cairo, where she is currently at work on her second poetry
collection, *Map of Time*.

Forms of Nausea

On my way to my desk, I stop by the chief editor's office to pitch an article about nausea, of which I had recently experienced various forms. A nausea stained with the suspicion of absence takes me by surprise as I wait for the elevator to come down, and permeates my soul on the ride up. It floats glaringly before me in the morning, on the faces flocking robotically towards their workplaces, heedless of their destination—and then I forget all about it on my way back. He says the idea is not quite right for a business magazine, and suggests alternative headlines for me to pursue: Maintaining Co-Worker Relations, Traits of the Ideal Employee, How to Rid Yourself of Daily Stress. I think of the many missing links, and all the intertwined links; of the words we have yet to say, and the words we will never say. Aloofly, I tell him that he has no idea what's going on. He nods his head in agreement and rambles on, as though what I had just said was as clear as day. I am pitching my idea to him with the same initial vigor when I notice the three little elephants on his desk, dancing ever so delicately.

Cancer

He knocks on our door in the morning, and runs off if anyone else responds, only to come back and knock until I let him in myself. I greet him with the sweetest good morning, and as we sip milk tea, he says nothing. He points to the dolls stacked on my bookshelves until I pull them down; he lays them out around him, before getting up to pull open the apartment door, only to make sure that leaving is permitted. When he returns, he has no idea what to do with all these dolls, so he unlatches the door and leaves. He thinks that the moon hanging above my bed is the same moon that hangs in the sky; that I spread my wings every night to haul it here, all to place it in his hands, and leave it sealed in his fist. Samer, my neighbor, has decided to name the malignant tumor that has afflicted his grandmother: *wawa*. Perhaps scientists should address this miscommunication, or else consider renaming all things as per Samer's dictionary.

SAMIRA NEGROUCHE

Translated by Nancy Naomi Carlson from French

I was first introduced to Samira Negrouche by Patrick Williamson, the curator of a feature on francophone poets published in *The High Window*, who asked me to translate one of her sequences of poems written in Algerian French. I was intrigued by the dream-like tone she created through the use of simple language looping back on itself in unique patterns to describe her anchoring idea that 'all life is movement.' The selection you're reading here comes from *Solio* (forthcoming from Seagull Books), which features complete translations of Negrouche's *Quai 2/1: A Three-Axis Musical Score* and *Traces*. The selection represents the final poems in *Quai 2/1*, with its haunting final stanza. The beings in Negrouche's surrealist universe inhabit movement, the borders of borders, and timeless space.

Opposite: An Algerian woman stood upright with her arms crossed smiles into the camera, against a background of tightly packed shelves of books. She wears tortoiseshell glasses, a turtleneck and a necklace with a large pendant.

Excerpts from Quai 2|1

I move forward
in the river moving forward
I'm rooted in movement
time passes through me
beings pass through me
they are me
I am them

I'm rooted in movement
when I dive
I resurface
when I arrive
I'm already far

*   *   *

I'm rooted in movement
my steps don't land
they dance
in the elsewhere

I'm rooted in movement
but when I'm rooted
in movement
I unroll
the horizon.

* * *

I've been gifted
to live
what
in the white dawn
awakens.

MEENA KANDASAMY

Meena Kandasamy's latest work, *The Book of Desire*, is a translation of the *Kāmattu-p-pāl*, a 2000-year-old song of female love and desire written in Tamil by the poet Thiruvalluvar. Although hundreds of male translations of the text have been published, it has also only ever been translated by a woman once before.

Sana Goyal interviews Meena Kandasamy on her feminist and decolonial intervention in and reclamation of the *Kāmattu-p-pāl*.

SG: Working on this translation, and living with this text, for decades—what was the process like for you, and what kept you coming back?

MK: My first encounter with this text was as a teenager—and like a lot of Tamil schoolchildren, learning it by rote. Obviously, that's the kind of age when you realise that the love poetry sections in the Tamil original of the *Tirukkural* has a vibe of its own, it's quite biased—but the translations were archaic, overwrought, and lacking that specific je ne sais quoi of the Tamil universe. I do not think I had any illusions of grandeur at that tender age, I never thought I would someday have the confidence, capability, and coolness to take on this text as a translator.

Also, the *Tirukkural* is not a book, it is THE book of Tamil society. How would I find the courage to imagine myself as doing anything with it? Everyone who touched it so far was a stalwart, a historical legend, all kinds of absolute literary or political figures... I did not envision this as a book at the beginning. My first kural translation happened in December 2010, when we were at Adishakti in Pondicherry and part of a Literature Across Frontiers workshop,

---

Opposite: An Indian woman with long highlighted hair looks over her left shoulder, back at the camera. She wears dangly circular earrings and a black coat.

and were all trying to produce work that was multilingual poetry in translation. Then in 2013 I started doing a few from the beginning of the Kamathuppaal section. There are 250 kurals in all, and it has taken ten years to bring it to completion; each kural is a poem in two lines, so all of this is not a lot of work. The idea of making this a book came during the pandemic. I had a reality check, understanding that as much as I loved the long-form fiction I was working on, this was the most disastrous moment to embark on it. So, I switched priorities. Every kural was portable that way: first I had the benefit of knowing them by memory, and secondly, there were about seven metremes/two lines, so it could be carried around and done on your phone in a notes app.

SG: In your introduction you've voiced reservations about writing the introduction — about contextualising the work instead of letting it speak for itself, stand on its own. How did you approach this dilemma, maintain that balance, without explaining or simplifying the text, the Tamil language, and larger literary culture as writers and translators from the 'Global South' are often expected to?

MK: Yes, it was not easy. but I had to decide one way or the other. In the end, I realised that the work would always speak for itself, and that the kuralo would live far longer and last into many more centuries irrespective of the contexts in which they are read, received, or remembered. So, I decided that situating the text would not affect the integrity of the work in any manner; it would not subtract from its charm. And that is so important in this day and age because it is not one of these dead classical texts that gets only taught at university, for example. Even today, we are having debates around the text, its author, its import in the political spectrum in my state—and for scale, it is a state of more than sixty million people. So, in many ways, the text becomes a part of political discourse. It becomes a rallying point, a counter-cultural weapon against Hindutva-Hindi hegemony even as it has been installed as the centrepiece of Tamil identity/culture over millennia.

I did not think of myself as a Global South writer, I am wary of such positioning especially when I've lived in London, taught at NYU, and my work (as a writer) resists such convenient appropriation. I increasingly feel both awkward and annoyed by such neat flattening. The Global South we speak about—in India for instance, we have such a caste system inside the academia, brutal Brahmin hegemony—what do I have to share with such academics? Nothing whatsoever. I finished my PhD more than a dozen years ago but I've never had an academic job in India. The gatekeeping here is nauseous. I think this system is fucked up. I've taught abroad, so the barrier here is not merit or qualification—the caste system is a major stink. 'Global South' is a nice term that perhaps allows many entrenched Indian Brahmin academics to occupy some sort of victimised position, but please, I'm not interested in that sort of positioning, and see several of them as upholding the status quo, perpetuating caste discrimination and oppression. Not my monkeys, not my circus.

My aim was to do justice to the text, to not only leave the text out there, but to document both the process of my translation and the history of the text itself so that everyone (any race, colour, culture) could read and understand and take away the politics in which this text has survived and exalted itself.

I hope it reads into a renewed interest in both translations from the Tamil, and voices writing in English/Tamil from the Tamil landscape. I do not think one book can change the way the world operates, but even if it shifts things a millimeter, I would consider it a success that something has been achieved.

SG: This is a bit of a double question. As someone who has translated poetry and fiction, and as a poet yourself, what was so special about working on this project in particular? For example, with your translation of Salma's *Women Dreaming*, you've spoken about the close, collaborative relationship between author and translator…

MK: Yes, but that relationship with Salma, if I may dare to call it an intergenerational friendship, was forged as a result of translating her work, and it was not something that existed before. Almost all of the texts which I have chosen to translate have been picked up because I identify with the politics that the author and the text represent. The same applies to Salma. With *The Book of Desire* I was aware of the politics of the text quite broadly, and somehow discussing aspects of it (first feminist translation, the political centrality of the text to the Dravidian movement in Tamil Nadu) were factors that I found worthy enough to help situate the text. The driving force in this case was not merely the political urgency but the way these words spoke to me, how it always seemed so personal and so specific and so tailored to what I was/had been through—when in fact these were universal lines.

With every writer, I did the translation with the absolute awareness that in English they wouldn't sound like I would—because stylistically our works/aesthetics were worlds apart. With the *Tirukkural*, obviously there was no way I was capable of composing one kural in Tamil, but I knew that if/when it was rendered in English, the love poetry would sound exactly like me. It felt like writing my own poems: that sense of exaggeration, that sense of wallowing in pain, that sense of longing. This is definitely the book I have most loved to inhabit.

SG: You've spoken elsewhere about this feminist, de-colonial translation as a 'circuit-breaker'. In your introduction you say that we need to 'widen the scope of what colonialism is', to look not always to western colonisers, but dark forces closer to home. Can you elaborate?

MK: I think this is an entire interview all by itself! To be brief, resisting internal colonialism (rather, resisting non-European colonialism) has been at the heart of Tamil resistance. Beginning in the 1930s when we had the first anti-Hindi agitations in the state, to the 1960s when the army had to be called in to suppress the wave of agitations against Hindi—there is a rich, documented history. It was not just this imposition of language, but it was a lot of incursions (beginning with temples, prayers, the language of prayers, the right of priesthood, all of it). Yes, we have suffered the consequences of British colonialism and English language unseating the mother tongue here, but we have waged greater struggles. When India was organised on linguistic lines, we had a separate state of Bihar, Rajasthan, Madhya Pradesh (everywhere because non-Hindi languages were spoken). Today, these languages have been destroyed, maimed, not allowed to flourish and have been adopted into the fold of Hindi. It is important to remember this.

SG: Can you talk a little about what you say in the introduction: that 'we need to weaponise the words we choose'. How can translation, in particular, help do this? And what three words would you choose to describe *The Book of Desire*?

MK: I was too much in love with the text when I kept translating it—and even then it was not difficult to see how over the centuries the text under male translators and commentators had been butchered from being a text celebrating female desire into a text upholding the idea of chastity. That was so shocking. Somewhere Tiruvalluvar would be writing about love pangs that cause pain, and

Parimelalagar, the 12th century commentator would come and say, 'Chastity, which is dearer than life itself'. Aha! That's how patriarchy scores. Or elsewhere the original would use a word like 'nirai' meaning fulfilment and containment, but the translators would call it spotlessness or chastity or something along those lines, evidently turning the text on its head. It was about female autonomy, and et voila, you have made it into a text about controlling women! You see that time and again, all of these insidious ways into which patriarchal readings have crept into the text and solidified their position there. So, I went into it, trying to break these shackles. So my weaponisation of the words I chose was a direct counter to how the text had been subverted over the ages. I had to undo all of this.

Three words: Longing. Sensuous. Dramatic.

CHEN XIANFA

Translated by Li Hai from Chinese

Chen Xianfa, born in Anhui in 1967, is one of China's most esteemed poets and currently Chairman of Anhui Federation of Literary and Art Circles. Chen graduated from Fudan University in Shanghai in 1989. He has published dozens of books of poetry, which include *A Past Life* (2005), *Writing Inscriptions with a Pure Heart* (2011), *The Problem of Raising Cranes* (Taiwan, 2015), and *Poems in Nines* (2017), as well as a collection of essays, *Notes on Black Pond Dam* (2021). He has received many poetry prizes, including the Lu Xun Literature Prize, China's prominent national literary award. His works have been translated into English, French, Russian, Spanish, and Greek. Chen aims at combining the beauty of classical Chinese poetry with modern aesthetic perception and sensibility.

The Acme of Order

In prison I took pleasure in practising headstands.
On my hands as I stood, the mountains had to follow suit.
Behind the bars, the prison guards' faces were dangling down.
The tiger in the distance
Couldn't help but appear upside-down. All through the autumn,
I kept staring at its bottomless throat.

MOHAMMAD-ALI SEPANLOU

Translated by Siavash Saadlou from Persian

Mohammad-Ali Sepanlou (1940–2015) was one of the unsung poets of his generation. His poems encompass an impossibly wide array of themes, from urban life to civil strife, from the treachery of politics to the trajectory of wars, and from erotic fantasies to faraway galaxies. The language in his work is disarmingly delicate, and distinct in its blend of clarity and confusion. In his poem, 'Mosaddegh', Sepanlou beautifully captures the pathos in the story of Mosaddegh's fall from grace. The tone of Sepanlou's voice is no different than that of Whitman in his oft-quoted lines from 'O Captain! My Captain!'. Choosing the word 'careworn'—as opposed to numerous other synonyms—was extremely important as it highlights Mosaddegh's genuine concern for the fate of his homeland.

Mosaddegh[1]

Let us spread your message with our
silent eyes. Let your walking stick,
with our patience, slowly grow
flowers on your bucolic burial place.
Let the tuneful waters running
under the old tree forever eulogise
about freedom.

Woe to the augury of death that knew
just how to bring about the undoing of
gray-haired men and larger-than-life heroes,
clawing at the careworn throat of the most
patriotic orator of our time.

Be aware that a life this vain,
from home to the crowded office,
from the winery to the water seller,
from one thirst to another, is our way
of sacrificing our souls, but the longing
for badges of honor was never
conceived in our minds.

Let our fruitful silence rise up
and blossom on the first branches.
This is a way of being in a land
bereft of bearings to nurture
old men of sagacity.

1 Mohammad Mosaddegh (1882–1967) was the 35th Prime Minister of Iran
whose government was overthrown by a CIA-led coup d'état in 1953.

RAFIQ SANDEELVI

Translated by Abid Raza from Urdu

Rafiq Sandeelvi is a noteworthy name in the context of modern poetics of Urdu language. He has developed a unique narrative for human life and relationships in today's complex world. His reader might require more than a cursory glance to pause and ponder between the lines and phrases in order to get to the deep layers of intent and meaning. His topics are often diverse and his style is unusually mature with frequent subtle symbolism and eloquent artistry. A brilliant portrayal of human existence and behavior in the modern world, his poetry is well loved by academia, literati and common readers of Urdu language alike. His poem 'Listen to the Prophecy' is about the impact of environmental degradation and global climate change.

Listen to the Prophecy

Listen to the prophecy—
half of my body will turn into a tree,
a blood-thirsty tree,
from roots up to spikes.
Listen to my prophecy—
if a bird ever chirps on my branches,
it will be desiccated in an instance
like it never had a breath of life in it.

Listen to the prophecy—
half of my body will turn into a tree
and the other half will melt
into night's dense water
poisonous from drop
to deluge.
Listen to the prophecy—
If a bird ever dips in
It will turn to mush.

O lively birds
soaring in heavenly horizons
from now on, stay out of my reach.
Rest in the silky nests of your bodies,
the exuberant twigs and tendrils of
your wings and feathers.
Listen to the prophecy—

VERÓNICA JAFFÉ

Translated by Gabriel Araujo from Spanish

Since the best theory about poetry and translation cannot be universal, its writing is circumstantial and will depend on the moment and place, just as poetry, if honest, knows that it is a translation of the words and images of others. (VJ)

Excerpt from 'Theoretical Poems'

What does translation
hide and
will never reveal
but the real or forked
tongue,
my pure and simple
tongue?

*

Hiding deep in the forest
of tongues lurks
the original so it does not have to
reply to the foreign
translation
that with its name cries.
Echo will reply,
that distant nymph,
from within
her own forest.

CALL THE SEA A POET

Focus on Malta

ANTOINE CASSAR

Translated by the poet from Maltese

On conventional north-up maps, when not hidden behind the letter
M or a circled star, Malta appears to be shaped like a fish: small
fry adrift in a large blue battlefield, but also, of course, an ancient
Christian symbol. Beyond popular imagination, the south-western
bulge of the main island might rather suggest the shape of a whale,
linking to the Jonah Complex: a society that fears becoming itself,
that has spent three generations at pains to comprehend and accept
its Mediterranean identity (somewhere between southern European
and Maghrebi, and/or vice-versa).

Rotate the map—east-up—and the main island morphs into
a long face that appears to be choking. In overdeveloped Malta,
solitude is difficult to find; one might look for it on the coast, staring
out toward the horizon, yet the sense of being watched (and judged)
remains. Paradoxically, many Maltese report feeling alone in their
claustrophobia. How to escape the belly of the whale? Spend too long
on an island, and the more you pine to leave, the more difficult
leaving becomes.

Opposite: A Maltese man with a beard and a cap smiles into the
camera, wearing a black shirt with a ship in front of a moon as it
crests over the waves. Photo: Zvezdan Reljić

I looked up

The world begins in Qrendi and ends in Xlendi:
this island is a planet in a dark sea,
the sun circles it—not vice-versa—
illuminating her alone, whilst the moon
goes on shifting the horizon back and forth.

I looked up to stop feeling dizzy:
I saw a net of stars wrapping everything,
now and again tightening so as to remind us
that not even galaxies away from this island
can there ever be a way out.

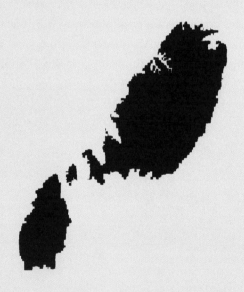

Above: Royalty-free image taken from vectorstock.com, a silhouette of the
island of Malta, rotated upside-down.

CLAUDIA GAUCI

Translated by Albert Gatt from Maltese

The poems in *Max-Xatt tat-Tamarisk* explore themes such as
childhood and nostalgia, relationships, motherhood, love and the
environment. The title of each poem is a question which answers the
whole poem itself. The poems can be seen as one answer to the
question and, in a way, may entice the reader to come up with her
own way of seeing things. The poem chosen for this magazine, 'Shall
we rest a bit before we catch the last ferry back?' takes the reader
along a very local topography. The poem evokes the sounds and
moods of a typical hot and humid summer from which the poetic
voice emerges subtly melancholic and restless.

Shall we rest a bit before we catch the last ferry back?

So yes, one hour to go before we make our way down to Imġarr.
Drawn out as long as it'll allow, our lazy Qala afternoon
tastes of figures-of-eight dunked in mugs of Nescafé.
We waver—what time shall we catch the ferry?—as the ships
glide like games of beads across the channel.

They've come to a sluggish end, these summer-scorched days
of restless nights in spasms stirring on the bedsheets,
the streetlight a peeping Tom between the shutters.
I can't be bothered to get up and close them,
so I huff and curse the moon and turn my back to it.

Through the unyielding dark that still lurks at the window
I listen to the crickets tearing summer to shreds.
In the field across the street, a cloudy mare ducks her head
into the falling dusk, her tail swishing the brutal summer away.
By late afternoon
the gathering cumulus heralds another dreamless night.

On the terrace in the evening
the loudspeaker jolts awake
and I'm a blur in the ice-slicked glass, moving to its rhythm.

Opposite: A Maltese woman with shoulder-length hair grins into the
camera, her arms folded over a black top.

MARIA GRECH GANADO

Translated by the poet from Maltese

A retired lecturer in English, I am a graduate of the Universities
of Malta and Cambridge, and have published seven collections of
poetry in Maltese or English, with an eighth in English launched
in June 2023.

Amongst various awards, I have received a D.Litt (Honoris Causa)
from the University of Malta for my contributions to literature,
including playing a major role at the beginning of Malta's annual
Mediterranean Literature Festival, now in its 19th year.

I have three children and three grandchildren.

'The Wave' ('Il-Mewġa'), translated by myself, is from one of my
four Maltese collections, *Fil-Ħofra Bejn Spallejha* (*In the Dip Between
Her Shoulders*, 2005), and tells metaphorically of a woman's frustrated
failure to communicate her overpowering emotions.

The Wave

A number of times I'd set out to search
for the wave that sweeps us all away.

It was because of this I stripped you naked
then threw your clothes haphazardly
upon a rock with mine—
and on tiptoe under the moon
whispered to you between our kisses
of a salt door within the wave.

You pulled me close but waited in vain
and, feeling cold, you dressed and left

while I remained, licking the salt
around my mouth with a dry tongue,
still waiting for the wave
that sweeps us all away.

IMMANUEL MIFSUD

Translated by Ruth Ward and Immanuel Mifsud
from Maltese

'All Roads Lead to Rome' captures the slippery nature of time: its
relentless onward propulsion; its infinite circularity. Immersed in
impermanence, we craft our own illusions of control—for better or
for worse. Who has not heard the footfall of present-day gladiators
'ready for blood'? Malta, like Rome, has seen its own millennia of
change. Towers and traffic jams smother swathes of what was once
fertile soil. Rome fell. What have we learned?

All Roads Lead to Rome

As we walk amidst
cars, trams, and scooters
in the same whereabouts where
legionnaires, centurions, and gladiators marched
ready for blood,
we indulge discussing time
without noticing it is discussing us
with itself.

ABIGAIL ARDELLE ZAMMIT

In English

At a natural history museum, in a town in the northeast of Iceland,
I discovered the stuffed carcass of a raven, its heart, mutilated,
invisible, but bearing, according to the caption, the secret language of
all birds. And because folktale speaks in many tongues, that absent
heart became a way of translating politics into art, a symbol for the
brutal silencing of the Maltese journalist Daphne Caruana Galizia.
So it happens that having searched for months, you discover your
subject very far from home, perhaps, like me, in the mirror of a
frozen lake. Soon after, the other Daphne texts appeared—
#wearedaphne—blackout erasures based on translations from
Ovid's *Metamorphoses*, all of which tell and retell a story that
weeps as it sings.

Two Landscapes, with Woman

For Daphne Caruana Galizia—
assassinated 16th October 2017.

i

Ólafsfjarðarvatn. Ice cracks beneath
my boots, fails to blot out the memory

of a woman, blasted—burnt pieces of
what she used to be

assembled for the autopsy.

There are crooks everywhere you look now.
The situation is desperate.
https://daphnecaruanagalizia.com/

ii

Firs in mutiny against the snow.

The cliff-edge ridged with steel blue,
outstretched hooves, rigor mortis.

It's the carcass of a sheep still woolly,
herbivorous cavity exposed.

Cavity: 'a hollow place, empty space in the
body,' 1540s, from Middle French 'cavité',
from Late Latin 'cavitatem' 'hollowness', from
Latin 'cavus' 'hollow'.

iii

I skate to ravens
cawing on each aerial.

Their beaks must reek
of fish gut. The crystal lake

conceals. Brings salt and herring,
then takes away. They say

to know all things, kill a raven—
cut out its heart, keep it

under the tongue—

Hrafn (Corvus corax)　　FUGLAMÁL
*Vilji maður skilja fuglamal má drepa hrafn
skera úr honum hjartað og geyma I munni
sér undir tungunni.*

ALBERT MARSHALL

Translated by John Consiglio from Maltese

This is a translation of the Maltese original—'L-Istorja tal-Gifa'—as written and published in Albert Marshall's collection *Poeziji 1964–2019*. Besides being a well known poet, theatre director, and writer in his own right, Marshall has for many years been the head of Malta's Arts Council, the national body responsible for cultural development and the arts on the beautiful Mediterranean island of Malta. The poem is a soliloquy by the 'wise fool' who questions both himself and his close interlocutors about what he feels they should know about his, and their, ability to catch moments and ideas as they rapidly pass on in life and, perhaps more importantly, as life moves towards its end.

The Fool's Tale

You know that tale about the fool
who loves people... and Turkish delight

Were I not a human
I wouldn't be shy to admit to you
that I am that fool

I would drop like the crucified and rise again
free from all
from everyone

I'd have a meal for your sakes
on dishes facing downwards
bedecked in black

And I'd bid you goodbye
just now
before it is too late
today for the few
tomorrow for nobody
before another hour brings in winter
and before summer's glean of dust
brushes from my eyes
like whitewash from the ceiling of winter's room
where my bedside chair rises from the old floortiles
with neatly bedecked on its back
a silken shirt
tasting of humidity.

I'd have acted a majestic exit
from the theatre floor
pirouetted in the doorway
and blown a Judaic kiss
to the cultural prophets in the first rows.

The picnic of this moment I'd have reversed
and raised the gestalt of my kids round the chair
in my rain room
that salty gestalt
as their arms reach out hungry for their mother.

You all know the fool's tale—
the one who loves people and Turkish delight

'Cause me... I don't.

NORBERT BUGEJA

Translated by Irene Mangion from Maltese

'Memento Mori' forms part of a poetic cycle in which, two decades
after the tragic demise of his mother, Norbert Bugeja reaches into the
fraught silences of time to summon forth the echoes of a conversation
that ended abruptly, in the midst of one summer afternoon. Poetry
here returns as a language stolen from the erosion of memory: letters
of salt burning in the flesh of remembrance, the ephemeral syllables
of a nation that persists on the cliff-edge of disrupted youth, half
of an island scratched into the morning sand. Bugeja rummages
in sequences of rhythm, metaphor, image and synaesthesia to
capture the mood of years across which forgetting, as much as
remembrance, became a condition for surviving amid the ruins
of an interrupted bond.

Memento Mori

Once her eyes have taken in the view, she rises,
and amid the eroded prose of the stones,
figures out where she is—she's a little late. Just a little.
She can't tell how the morning sped by, except for the dread
of the coffee trembling on the edge of the table.
Get me out of this temple, she'd said—
don't bring me back before it has collapsed.
Sometimes, from the other end of the day,
I still wave to her. Sometimes, I still dream
of Morocco slumbering on her lap: an invitation
to take to the road and pray that the tattered nets
of her lips will not tumble into me.
Where did the winds go after scattering us
all over the islands, like black letters lying flat
on the listless tongue of the night? A fleeting thought
tethered to one thing alone, this stone—
a theatre adrift on the perfumed ankle of time.

KARINA FIORINI

In English

Karina Fiorini's writing is made up of scraps of fragments, teasing rhythms, subtle colours. It criticises, alludes to pain, to exhilaration and to being human. 'Grigal's mouth', whilst representing the wind, focusses on the Maltese Islands, as it makes parallel their force and that of the sea. The poem invokes the 'migrant crisis', the finite limestone resource, fish-farms' impacts, flooding and lack of water catchment measures, and general political inaction. Simultaneously, this context is pelted by inhabitants' timeless routines, mirrored in life and death, in addition to the echoing lines; a reminder of daily, repetitive local church bells and the forgotten creed. Governance whorls are busted by 'Grigal's mouth''s subversive slant—the people rise against the old governing cult.

Opposite: A Maltese woman standing on a rocky outcrop, with the sea behind her, smiles into the camera. Her hair is whipped forward by the wind and she wears a black shawl and tinted sunglasses.

Grigal's Mouth

Grigal's mouth shakes
hair-knots free, shifts brain
cells, hurricanes roach
bodies on door steps

still, the peroxide head
pegs a smile on dizzy clothes

still, the abbey's nun got a habit,
walks on, holds her veil,

| it is time | it is time | it is time | to recall |
| it is time | it is time | it is time | to recall |

that in the Med sea, bodies thrown
off-kilter, whorl in currents
as the Grigal mouths
knapweeds, spindrifts limestone,
bells howl in Żabbar

| it is time | it is time | it is time | to recall |
| it is time | it is time | it is time | to recall |

that across villages, bold
waters run off roofs, coffins float
in Qormi, cross-eyed rain pelts farmed
sea bream in Xemxija streets

still, the girl pencils pronouns
at the Valletta funeral parlour

still, the gale wakes
Momus from slumber

as Grigal mouths tensions
against the old cult

KARL SCHEMBRI

Translated by Miriam Calleja from Maltese

Karl took a photo in Eastern Ghouta, outside Damascus, Syria, some years ago. The neighbourhood was the site of a cruel siege and was cut off from basic supplies. He was in a school, meeting children after the siege was lifted, when he ventured out to take in the surrounding destruction. He captured an image of this solitary man walking with a bicycle in a street full of houses with no facades left. This image would come back to him with greater force as war broke out on Ukraine and he wrote his poem 'Fejn ħallejtha r-rota meta ħrabt?' With this poem, Karl wanted to remind our leaders of this unknown man with a bicycle who might die as a direct result of their decisions.

Above: As in the Note above, by Miriam Calleja, a 'solitary man walking with a bicycle in a street full of houses with no facades left.' He wears pants and a shirt, and is walking the bicycle from the right-most part of the image to the left.

Where'd you leave your bicycle when you fled?

You left everything behind,
carried a blanket, some nappies, your daughter
crossed the river under the wrecked bridge,
walked in the rain and drought
on ground ready to swallow you whole,
on seas the colour of dark
far from home,
far from everything you left behind:
the graduation certificate in art from the technical institute
all the family photos – including yours at age five wearing a
    blue blazer,
your childhood bicycle which you kept to give to your children
    one day,
the stamp collection,
the love letters from your first girlfriend, hidden in a shoebox,
a suitcase that travelled with you and your father when you didn't have
    to flee.
Where did you leave the suitcase?
Where is the door you locked?
Did you leave through some alley in the old city of Mosul?
Or through the seashore at Hodeida?
Or maybe you waded through the barrage of rubbish from aliens in
    Sheikh Jerrah?
Did you by any chance cross the underground tunnels in Gaza that
    take you to the mouth of the Egyptian Pharaoh?
Or perhaps were you closer to us? Like us?
What colour are your daughter's eyes?
Recently a throng arrived from Kyiv.
Those take priority, those are more like us.

Those need to come in
Never mind that until yesterday we only let in women working in
    exclusive clubs for slick traffickers.
Never mind that until this morning we were still trying to fleece them
    in quarantine while we sold passports to butchers with golden
    serrated knives.

Where'd you leave your bicycle when you fled?
In some torn-up road in Tripoli
or in some civilized European city?
You understand that these are important questions. It is necessary
    that we ask.
You understand that not everyone who leaves everything behind
    deserves our time.
There are complicated issues, you know:
Do you prefer kebabs or widow's soup?
Do you eat rice with a fork or with your hands?
When you kill someone do you make the sign of the cross or say
    Allah hu akbar?

Sit down – we'll take some notes before we commit ourselves.
We won't take too much time, nowadays we've learned to recognise
    the chaff.
We will soon be able to let you know whether your atrocities align
    with our compassion.
You understand that we've become efficient at weighing things out:
there's Apartheid and Apartheid
there's dictators and dictators
there's resistance and resistance
there's a killer and a killer
there's us and them

and you, and your daughter,
and the form that needs to be filled in
and details on your skin and kin
and remind me,
where did you leave your bicycle when you fled?

JESMOND SHARPLES

Translated by the poet from Maltese

The poem 'Denouement' is a declarative statement by a people
who are fed up with their corrupt premier and the associated poor
governance. The message in the poem has a universal implication and
it does not refer to any particular country. The poem, whose concrete
form strengthens its declarative nature, purposely overutilises
techniques such as rhyme and alliteration, alluding to the 'chime
of a billion dimes', the flowing abundance of money from such
illicit activity. The Denouement at the end reveals to the reader the
denouncement of such political grime and slime, and surprisingly
also the poetical rhyme which is abundantly used in the poem.

Opposite: A Maltese man on a boat looks into the camera, wearing
rectangular tinted glasses and a black zip-up fleece. Sunlight is cast onto
the left side of his face; behind him is the sea and a rocky mountain.

Denouement

We, the people announce that
we deem it prime time
to denounce and renounce
all the grime, slime and crime
of the prominent Premier of the Isle of Sublime
whose dream of begriming the chime of a billion dimes
is now in tatters and for all that matters
it's time to denounce and renounce
this toxic and caustic lime,
grime, slime
(and rhyme).

GLEN CALLEJA

Translated by Albert Gatt from Maltese

In the hierarchy of smells that announce new beginnings, the smell of
a freshly painted house is at the very top. The harsh smell of volatile
chemicals comes wafting assertively the minute you enter the house.
It engulfs you. The place feels clean, new even, free from old troubles.

This literary collage is a response to the compulsion to seek fresh
beginnings and the technologies, symbolic or otherwise, we employ
to express hope and to cancel and forget trauma.

The government in your house

The government in your house
smells of fresh paint.

It takes samples of your headaches,
for filing purposes, it takes samples
of this newfound cleanliness.

Question: *Those flying ants, do they still give you trouble?*

Yes, I say, they give me trouble still, those flying ants,
especially in the evening,

inside my eye sockets
they're drawn to the light.

Now every window's open.
Let in some fresh air.

AARON AQUILINA

In English

This poem plays with my hyperawareness of language, a characteristic shared by most 'non-native' speakers of English who nonetheless deploy it daily. The persona retreats from their loss or pain through an interrogation of grammar, an almost absurd reaction, but perhaps this linguistic manipulation offers some access to an emotional reality that could not be articulated otherwise.

Despite Maltese being my mother tongue, it is nonetheless within the rules and strictures of my second language that I find the tenses (if not the words) to express, in this poem, some sort of fatalistic hope. These gaps in my languages, a constant play of meaning and its lack, are here utilised almost ironically in an attempt to mirror the gaps between what is and what may be.

Conditional

I miss you conditionally.

What would he say if he were sitting here?
If he were with me, I would not feel this way.
How much he would have loved this weather.

I remember rehearsing the conditional tense,
a square of children neatly packed before me
as I gesticulated, drew lines of time
explaining the possible but never true.

If they were to win the lottery,
asking them what they would do
was a dependable question,
though it always resulted in formulaic phrases
and unimaginably boring billionaires.

Conditionals that express facts:
When you are not here, I miss you.
Conditional probability:
If you were still here, I would be happy.
Conditional improbability:
If you and I abandoned our life, we'd find a new one.
Conditional impossibility:
Had you stayed, I would not have felt bereft.
Had you died, I could accuse time of such theft.

RITA SALIBA

Translated by the poet from Maltese

The poem is about the dilemmas a mother goes through as she sees her daughter growing up. Will she be forgiven for hurting her child as she tight plaited her hair? Being there for her child can be tiring, but watching her through adolescence can be tough. Motherhood can be a cycle of holding on and turning away from a child's behaviour. It's about the urge to resist change. Sometimes letting go is often not a passive choice but one that requires time and effort. But what if it was too soon to let go? Will the anguish and sense of guilt get washed by tears alone?

Letting go

I've plaited your hair
many times and you winced
not wanting to say a word
on our way to school.
You thought I was hurting you on purpose
when I put plaster on your cut knee
the day you fell
from your new bicycle,
and a week passed before
you looked back to say
you're going for choir practice,
after I said no to a sleep over,
not even giving a thought
that I knew you were going somewhere else.
I shook my head when you put on that red dress,
then you changed into your jeans and T-shirt,
thinking I didn't notice the paper bag by the front door.
I watched you from the front window,
your long hair flapping as if to say goodbye to childhood.
You wept in my arms that night,
in that dress torn to shreds,
exposing your bruised thighs and bleeding shins.
You smothered your fear on my shoulder
and I think I heard you ask
why did I let go.

GIOELE GALEA

Translated by Abigail Ardelle Zammit from Maltese

Each poem in Gioele Galea's *Ilma—Water*—is a conversation between the soul and the Being from which it springs, and to which it hopes to return. Each word burns with a fire that bares it to its very essence. Each verse is water on the verge of turning into its other forms. Each poem is a minimalist sculpture ready to melt into metaphysical flux, which is why translating Galea's work is transformative and purifying. Having lived as a hermit for fourteen years, his poetic consciousness flows from and towards the same source, finding ways of expressing its spiritual turmoil through both poetry and hybrid prose memoirs whose journey is marked by an exquisite, almost unbearable tension.

41

You may glimpse
the rippling water
as it gathers light
in its lap.

You may light up
from within
and then you'll have to
open your blazing eyes.

You may
wait endlessly
and nothing happens.

Waiting,
you might merge
with the rocks
and sleep.

Opposite: A Maltese man with short hair and stubble gazes to the right in
a black high-collared coat.

44

Don't call it by any other name –

not before you've
seen it retreat
leaving behind
pebbles and sand,
dead seaweed, the broken
shells of cockles and mollusks –

not before.

These would be its scraps,
its poetry.

Thereafter, yes,
call the sea
a poet.

PRISCILLA CASSAR

Translated by Maria Grech Ganado from Maltese

The poem submitted was originally written in Maltese and published as 'Kollezzjoni' in *Leħen il-Malti XXXV* (2016)—a yearly publication of l-Għaqda tal-Malti, University of Malta, dating back to 1931. The poem was translated by the poet Maria Grech Ganado, who had encouraged me to write from the very start. It had been well received and it deals with wishing to keep the positive, intimate memories of a loved one alive even in his absence. I tend to write mainly love poems, but I have also written political ones. With one of the latter, titled 'Amal', I was a runner-up in the Adult Unpublished category of the Trócaire Poetry Ireland Poetry Competition 2020.

Collection

I wish I could steal
some of your breath
fold it gently
and save it,

pack the fingerprints
you play hide-and-seek with
upon my body,
in a casket cracked
by the warmth of the sun,

measure
the stroke of your tongue
tempting my breasts
and pour its weight into this casket
I've saved in my chest.

In this way, when the winds
race each other
to split one towards north
the other towards south

I can let out your breath
your fingerprints
and the stroke of your tongue,
air them
and wear them

even in your absence.

ADRIAN GRIMA

Translated by Albert Gatt from Maltese

'We are the Freed' is the last poem in a cycle of four inspired by the one-hundredth anniversary of Malta gaining self-government in 1921. Malta had been a colony of the British empire effectively since the beginning of the ninetenth century. After the bleak years following World War I and the bread riots of June 1919, the Maltese finally got their own administration, albeit with limited powers. In the first three poems the poet addresses his son who turned 21 in 2021; in the fourth, it is the son who addresses the father, proudly proclaiming what kind of Malta he believes in and is striving for.

We Are the Freed

You told me you're the son of '21

and this, the land of light and of those freed.

You told me you didn't want queens and kings,

for this land is no fiefdom ruled by lesser gods and we –

we are not grubs and flies.

You told me pedestals are built for saints

and towers for the detained and confined,

You told me there's no room for oligarchs and patriarchs.

That the sun will sing its song for North

and South.

You told me this land is for the living,

whatever their tone and tongue,

whatever their traits or visage;

land of carob trees and jujube.

This land is for the living, you said,

not for persons made of glass.

A land of open land and thyme,

of basil, rosemary and mint.

We exchange our views among the herbs,

you said,

exuded by the soil like mists of wonder;

we spend our mornings mapping out the ways

of hearts and minds,

we cross the middle sea

and come across in the tongues and idioms of creation.

This, you told me,

is a free land.

And we –

we are the freed.

Note: In 1921 Malta first gained self-governance.

ADRIAN GRIMA

Of Reach and Richness

The streets of Paris are a universe of languages. There's no way
of telling where they will come from and when they will brush by.
They come and go as swiftly as air, when earphoned or headphoned
androids walk past you, and speak to their alter ego as they stare
into their future. More often than not, the Mediterranean in me
has to make an extra effort to catch a whiff of the sounds. And then
attempt to identify at least the language family. But this doesn't
make these languages any less proud, any less determined to make
themselves heard.

There are languages everywhere in this cosmopolitan body, and
sometimes they are shrouded in the silence of what for me is a
northern European city. But they most certainly won't be silenced.
The city thrives in the semantics of its tongues, in the hues that come
with each one, every time it is uttered. Or should I say mouthed? It's a
strange verb, 'to mouth'. It's about uttering very clearly and distinctly.
And it carries a number of rather negative connotations, as in 'to be
all mouth'. However, to me, there's all the special physicality of
pronounced words that comes with 'mouthed'. It's the kind of
physicality that I'm drawn to when I don't know what the sounds
mean. Which is normally what happens to me on the streets of
Paris, on crowded trams, on trains on the metro. You end up sharing
intimate spaces, for a few long minutes, with people you don't
know, and will never get to know, until the next stop. Until the
doors swing open again to let out a wave of languages, and allow
a new battery to swarm in.

Opposite: A Maltese man in a grey suit jacket and collared shirt smiles
softly into the camera. He wears tinted rectangular glasses and is set
against a blurred park background.

I particularly love Arabic. Again, it's something very personal. And probably has partly to do with the fact that mine is a language of Arabic origins, with many of the characteristics you would associate with Arabic languages, especially those spoken on the street. It's perhaps because I can pick up some words here and there. Some individual words, I mean, not whole strings, but markers nonetheless. Perhaps it's because of the complicity of Maltese with Arabic, with various Arabics, in fact.

(There's French everywhere, of course. As I struggle to pick up words and expressions everywhere I go, even while I'm immersed, on a rare seat on the metro, in Justine Augier's *Sur les pouvoirs de la littérature*. I miss all the particular accents, well beyond my fraught French, yet I just enjoy being immersed in it.)

At the twice-weekly open market in the centre of Gentilly, where I'm staying this year, the many arabophone vendors try to sell me their fruit and veg in Arabic. Because that's what my complexion, my appearance tells them: that I probably come from North Africa, and speaking to me in my language, or the language of my family, of their country of origin, is an act of complicity, of friendship, of sharing something special. It creates community. It connects. It bonds. Sadly, I have to reply in French, for if I utter a couple of words in my language, they're going to release a string of Arabic that I'm not going to be able to deal with. That would come across as a betrayal. The man who betrayed his own language. His own community. The man who betrayed that initial verbal act of friendship. Because language is about creating encounters and relationships, sometimes fleeting ones, of course, but encounters nonetheless. No less than that which makes everyday life worth the trouble.

At the Maison de la Recherche of Inalco, the university of languages and civilizations, in rue de Lille, I listen to Maysa Ouarda

talk about the linguistic ideologies and language practices of the
Tunisians of Sfax ('*Idéologies linguistiques et pratiques langagières des
Tunisiens de Sfax*'). I'm particularly engaged: my language is said to
have come from a central Mediterranean, local variety of Arabic
spoken in Tunisia around the eleventh century, and brought to our
islands by Arabs living in Sicily.

At one point, Ms Ouarda highlights the importance of the word
'barrani', the same word for 'foreigner', or more precisely, 'outsider',
in my language. In Sfax, 'barrani' is not only a person from outside
one's community, or family: it is also someone who does not speak
my language, with my accent, my inflections. The concepts of
'territory', 'the in-group', even 'home', are therefore outlined by
words, by the way they are uttered. They are that important.

As she elaborates on the significance of the concept of 'barrani',
I'm thrilled. This is someone I have never met, and will possibly
never meet again, who is using a word which is such an intimate part
of the culture and language that has shaped me. My 'barrani' is also
hers, and that of the people of Sfax and beyond, all the way to Paris.
It's uttered on the streets of Paris every day. 'My' community has
suddenly grown in size, reach and richness.

A few days later I watch an *avant-première* of the stunning
Moroccan film *Le bleu du Caftan* at the Institut du Monde Arabe,
and one of the words that I immediately connect with is 'bnin'. The
husband tells his terminally ill wife that the food she has cooked for
him is 'bnin'. Savoury. Palatable. Wholesome. It's said in the perfect
context, with the perfect tone of voice, as it would be in mine. I'm
so proud that I want to look around the theatre hall, to make sure
everyone knows it's my wholesome word too, my tone of voice,
my warmth. I can feel it in my flesh.

No other language can connect me to the contours of the

European Mediterranean island south of Sicily, Tunis and Algiers that I live in, to its rich history, to its complex present. No other language can make me walk the streets of Paris with a sense of identity, a sense of pride, and an insatiable curiosity about the languages people speak, what they tell me about the cultures we shape and inhabit.

My language makes me feel that I am someone, that I belong in a cultural skin within which I can claim a world. It reminds me that I have been graced with this warm pot of savoury words that has been feeding us for well over a thousand years, allowing us to constantly add new ingredients to feed the next generation.

In this rich universe of languages, only my language can do that.

NADIA MIFSUD

Translated by Miriam Calleja from Maltese

I've yet to read this poem in Maltese or English without getting gooseflesh. The lines almost say more in what they leave out. On the edges, nostalgia and desire are shoulder to shoulder, just like the couple in the poem. Mifsud steeps the sparse stanza in imagery that is as quiet as what follows the storm. And yet, drips, creaks, and kitten cries are interspersed with a haunting we only get a hint of. What would we know if we heard the hundred tales of Mifsud's 'you'?

A Maltese woman holding her head, tilts it to the left and smiles into the camera. She wears a floral shawl and a wristwatch.

rainshower

The rainshower stops
and this city suddenly looks changed.
It smells of wet stone
a damp stillness
undisturbed
except for the cry
of a kitten
wrapped in shivers
against the doorpost.
Sounds of water dripping,
of water pipes ticking.
Gratings creak beneath our feet.
(Someday I'll tell you
about our childhood games
in grandma's basement,
our laughter interrupted
by imagined ghosts.)
Your eyes also
hide a hundred tales.
With each step
our shoulders rub—
craving a dance.
A gust of wind swings
the suspended street lamps
from one side of the road
to the other
and with them
light swings in
reflected cobblestones—
tender as your voice.

NADIA MIFSUD

Translated by Luke Galea from Maltese

The poetry of Nadia Mifsud has always fascinated me. I can still recall the first time I read her work—it was on a flight back to Cologne, Germany, where I was living at the time, and I felt like I was straddling between two countries, two identities, two selves. I was impressed that I was reading poetry that captured these feelings and more, such as feelings of displacement, foreignness, being an outsider. Moreover, Nadia's contemporary work focuses on womanhood and motherhood.

The poem 'your fingers are again seized' is from the collection *meta tinfetaq il-folla* (when the crowd disperses) and was published by Ede Books in 2023. The poem 'your fingers are again seized' reflect Mifsud's concerns with the self, aging, and womanhood.

your fingers are again seized

your fingers are again seized
by a sudden fancy to undo
the squabbles knotted in(to) my hair.
(you remind me of my nan.) I tell you that
I don't know if you'll ever be able to find a way. (you
keep on insisting that it doesn't matter.)
I don't know how many women there are
in me (interested in counting them?), if
there really is a woman or else
a girl that aged before her time.
I've started to wear tiredness like an insole
in a shoe that's already tight. my vertebrae
feel terracotta—if you touch them,
they'll become crumbs. this city's tentacles
have almost caulked me into a ghost.
it's as if it has thrown me a ghost.

this bramble knot in my throat
is nothing bar the war
that I didn't know how to write.

and maybe you are the man that I least knew
how to love as I wanted.

MIRIAM CALLEJA

In English

Living in the US after a lifetime in Malta has made me reflect deeply on how my sense of self has been tied to place. Being perceived as 'unusual' or 'exotic', getting a sense of not fitting in, being in the midst of cultural differences, and being in a state of almost-constant translation pushed me to write on this 'new' identity. This poem in particular was written after attending a reading with Earth Poet and Eco-poet Fellow (2022) Nabila Lovelace, during the Magic City Poetry Festival in Birmingham, AL.

Rebel Dandelion

after Nabila Lovelace

I live inside a stranger
people describe in a way I don't understand.
I take her everywhere
even if she's more head than toes
or small of back. Even though most days
it seems I have not tamed her,
poems sticking from fleeting burrs,
wind settling in her eyes.
I pluck each dandelion dagger
a soulful giving cry.
I drag her out of a ditch.
She disobeys, talks to birds, translates trees,
doesn't forgive me.

CLARE AZZOPARDI

Translated by Albert Gatt from Maltese

This poem is about homelessness. Through the window, as leaves fall and the trees prepare for winter's sleep, we catch sight of a man sleeping on the pavement, covered in leaves. Leaves are all he has, they are all he feeds on. But what will happen when winter comes and there are no more leaves to conceal and protect him?

Opposite: A Maltese woman with curly hair, hoop earrings, a black shirt and glasses smiles into the camera. She is set against a plain grey background.

Excerpt from 'Autumn'

it could be the leaves
how they shower from the sky   how they blanket the ground
how they come down just for you
rain a rain o' foliage, a refreshing shroud of leaves
how you have nothing but words that speak more leaves
how they shield you   how you blow them off   how your face is
    suddenly revealed
how you spit them out of your mouth
there now, take a breath, breathe any way you can

it could be the leaves
your tongue one withered leaf a day
how they can't get the taste of you
how they overwhelm you
how they fill you up   how this is all you have   how it's all yours
the leaves now sodden now dry now
peeping through the window I can't see you
where have you gone?
take a breath let me catch a slight shift in the leaves

it could be you
how you're heaping at the pavement's edge   autumn piled up on you
how there's no other way you could be   how it chokes you
it could be
leaves from this autumn and the next
an autumn of leafy blankets
showers coming down on you
how it's not manna but it's still coming from the sky
I'm wondering
how you'll be
once winter edges in

MARIE GION

Translated by Kat Storace from Maltese

'back inside the film' is taken from Marie Gion's self-published debut collection, *għax id-drogi sbieħ* (*because drugs are beautiful*). The poems follow the narrator and their group of friends across various locations in Malta as they experience the emotional highs and come-downs of youth: ennui, drug-fuelled joy, desire, love, heartache and loss.

I first read the collection in 2013 when I was working as an editor for a local publication and was sent a review copy. Since then, I've lost count of the number of times I've re-read the poems, my edition well-thumbed and scribbled through with pencil. I've always loved the unselfconscious frankness of the poems; the way the language, characters, places conjure up a nostalgia for the Malta I grew up in. The writing itself is a masterclass in how the Maltese language as it is spoken can be poetry, too. This authenticity poses a particular challenge for translation into English.

back inside the film

In the morning,
the secret of what you did
turns you into a character in a play
as you look
at your mother's house
while sitting in the road.

Underneath the exhaustion, slumped
as though
you've been beaten up. Crying
on the inside,
while from the car
the house begins to open up before your eyes
and the gate and wall become impossibilities
in stone
and you,
alone, small
in the hand of fatigue,
feel
lost forever,
and you don't know how you're going to get up.
The house
towers over you
at the foot of a cliff.

Outside,
everyone
has begun to tick-tick into action.
From behind the glass,

the house
turns into a doll's house
and with a hiccup, all at once,
shrinks.

In the village piazza the bells
of guilt
are ringing out. The sun
gets in your eyes
as you look
upwards. A little
uncomfortable
behind the glass
tick-ticking and feeling
trapped.

Very slowly
you emerge and
lift your head
towards the bedroom windows
where your mother and father,
corpses,
still
haven't stirred.

Perhaps
some of the neighbours
throw you filthy looks
on their way to church in the morning,
and before them
you feel dirty.

Heavy
with fatigue
at the threshold, you lift up
your arm
to re-enter
the life that's become an act
to you. As usual,
you've forgotten
the empty water bottles
in the car,
but if your mother finds them,
she won't understand.

When finally
you get inside,
you catch
your face in the mirror
melting
like in *The Scream*. The car,
a Fiat Punto, is still
in the road. In this film
it's Sunday morning
in Żurrieq.

LEANNE ELLUL

Translated by Helena Camilleri from Maltese

Leanne Ellul is one of the most prominent contemporary writers in the Maltese Islands. A visit to Ireland incites a series of poems related to trees, acting as the foundation of the chapbook *Il-Manifest tas-Siġar* (tr: *The Tree Manifesto*), celebrating trees in different spaces in Malta and outside of it. Ireland is much greener than Malta, and while the poet was there, she was overtaken by the beauty and possibility of such hues. This inspired her to write an ode to old trees, in the form of 'Is-Siġar ta' Killarney' (tr: 'The Trees of Killarney'), the first poem in this cycle of tree poems. Ellul remarks on how an image of a willow tree diving, almost drowning, in the waters remained with her, allowing the poem to blossom.

the trees of killarney

as we're driving along the verge of the earth the trees hug us
the river flows beside us roots damp and diverted
telling us that the sun will rise while the road wants to part for us
they want to tell us that this earth is a different kind of green
that there are corners untreaded softness parted

the crows pecking grains off plains
and we have not yet seen the sunlight
amidst the trees, clouds

here the trees extend to one another and yearn
the roots drown in the river furled dark algae
our eyes hollow puddles do not sparkle
with them, with the trees, cowering away from us
not wishing to reach anywhere, reigning below and under us

the crows pecking grains off plains
and we have not yet glimpsed the sunlight
the river is withdrawing and dawn appears to be awakening-for-us

---

Opposite: A Maltese woman in a chequered scarf with short brown hair,
pearl earrings and a nose ring grins into the camera.

JASMINE BAJADA

Translated by the poet from Maltese

'harvest' is an autumnal poem set in a cultivated field in Gozo, an island in the Maltese archipelago. The persona observes the harvesting of sweet potatoes with a contemplative eye, lingering on the details of the agricultural act and her presence on the 'soft' soil.

The poem recounts the imparting of agricultual skills to a younger generation. The poetic space turns into an archive, preserving not just a personal experience but also a public memory, a Maltese tradition.

The poems collected in *wild tongue*, Bajada's forthcoming debut collection, are haunted by the Anthropocene. In 'harvest', the anxiety of having an impact on nature is expressed, but a consolation is found, at the end, in observing human tenderness.

'harvest' is dedicated to David.

Opposite: A woman looks directly into the camera, wearing a floral frilled dress, tied with a ribbon at the waist. She stands underneath a rose bush growing over a stone wall, wearing a gold heart-shaped necklace and matching earrings.

harvest

i observe you from afar —
three generations from different families,
pondering the next patch of soil.
tomorrow, each of your backs will ache, but different;
today, you bend over the soil in the same angle,
preparing to plunge the fork hoe's fangs.

a few digs ago, the old man had his shirt on,
singing 'L-Aħħar Bidwi f'Wied il-Għasel'[1].
he sang two lines then laughed —
looked at your hands in your big pair of gloves,
noticed the way you held the hoe.
that's not how you hold it, ħabib, he said —
and showed you how, so you could toss the leaves
to the side and reveal the rows of sweet potatoes.

*

too soft the soil
beneath my feet
that it unsettles me;
the footprints i leave
they are too big
i won't believe they're mine.
for a moment, i'm embarrassed —

1   'The Last Farmer in the Valley of Honey' is a Maltese song by New Cuorey.

until i come closer to you to see you
recognise the stalk from the mallow,
to open and pry the root from the earth.
out comes the earthworm; it bends back
into the dark. when you kneel down to brush
the soil off the potato, we loudly awe
at its size. it did not break under your blow
though it's easy to split it in half.

above your head, a cabbage butterfly
seizes another day in its delicate way.

OMAR SEGUNA

Translated by Alfred Palma from Maltese

Set against the backdrop of the long way back to 'normality' after the start of the pandemic, 'Now' is a positive poem about a better life in the future, in terms of relationships. It yearns for reconciliation after living separated lives, and a future together. Its metaphors describe the longing to move away from despair and isolation and from the mistakes of the past.

Omar Seguna, the poet, was born on the 25th July 1977 and has published three books: *Mal-Ħoss Qawwi tar-ragħad* (2001), *24, Triq Ħad-Dwieli* (2011) and *Xehir fis-skiet* (2019). Some of his writings have also appeared in several anthologies.

Alfred Palma, the translator, was born in Floriana, Malta, on September 8, 1939. He is best known for the complete and rhymed Maltese translation of Dante's *Divina Commedia*, which he finished in 1986, the Maltese translation of Shakespeare's play *Romeo and Juliet*, followed by other Shakespearean plays (as well as the Sonnets), and the Maltese translations of world famous works, written by great authors such as Oscar Wilde, Voltaire, D.H. Lawrence and Thomas Mann. A good number of the plays were staged at the local Manoel Theatre.

Now

Now that
the sea's begun to ebb and flow,
we can walk on along the shore,
where from afar we greeted ourselves,
from every side of the same waters
that left us both apart.
From an exhausting heat
onto a gentle breeze
which swayed
the almost shrivelled leaves,
and now the moon's begun to smile at us.

REVIEWS

Care as Interconnectedness

Something Evergreen Called Life, Rania Mamoun (translated by
Yasmine Seale), Action Books, 2023
Review by Mayada Ibrahim

Rania Mamoun wrote her radiant poetry collection *Something
Evergreen Called Life* as she grappled with depression and suicidal
thoughts. It was March 2020, the first Covid-19 lockdown had just
been announced, and she was still a stranger in a new country, having
been forced to flee political persecution in Sudan after more than a
decade of organising. *Something Evergreen* is the first book of poetry
to follow two novels, a collection of short stories, and a large body
of journalistic writing. Mamoun's pivot to poetry, startling in its
intimacy, foregrounds care and the need to cultivate it for oneself and
others. Her activism manifests as a disposition toward tenderness
and love. As she writes in an untitled poem:

the heart is the only refuge

Mamoun's is one of the most recognisable faces of the ongoing
mass uprising that erupted in 2018. In 2013, she co-founded the Wad
Madani resistance committee, one of approximately 8,000 self-
governed collectives that sprang up across Sudan. 'The peddler, the
artisan, the day laborer, the school-dropout, as well as the student
and the politically seasoned university graduate' teamed up to
organise in their daily confrontations with the security apparatus.[1]

1. Magdi El-Gizouli, 'Mobilization and Resistance in Sudan's Uprising: From
neighbourhood committees to zanig queens' https://riftvalley.net/sites/default/
files/publication-documents/Mobilization%20and%20resistance%20in%20
Sudan%27s%20uprising%20by%20Magdi%20el%20Gizouli%20-%20RVI%20
X-Border%20Briefing%20%282020%29_0.pdf

The committees assumed myriad forms which played a key part in toppling long-time dictator Omar Bashir in 2019. Today, in the face of war, they are coordinating medical care in bombed-out hospitals, providing shelter for the disabled community, and evacuating civilians from areas of intense fighting.

As a Sudanese person in the diaspora, I grew accustomed to seeing Mamoun on screens as I watched the endless footage of the millions' marches, the poems and chants, the injured and dead bodies being hauled away from the streets. I lived in a fractured state, my consciousness at odds with the world around me. Being a spectator— 'where there is no agency or possibility of intervention, where the only response available is a cognitive response,' as Anuk Arudpragasam puts it [2] —aggravated the feeling of dislocation that had always been there. So then comes this book, that speaks directly to that dislocation, and to the particularity of being a Sudanese in diaspora watching the revolution and subsequent war unfold. It overwhelmed me with a sense of recognition. Mamoun reflects on sorrows rooted in displacement, yet there is always a sense of connection, of being held.

> leisurely, as if all time
> were mine
> I am—
> afloat in a field of color
> in the vastness of seeing

Something Evergreen was not conceptualised as a book. It was born out of an attempt to curb the isolation of the pandemic. Mamoun and artist Diane Samuels, co-founder of City of Asylum, a residency

2. Sri Lankan Tamil novelist Anuk Arudpagasam has produced some of my most treasured writing on exile. https://lareviewofbooks.org/article/the-jarringness-of-witnessing-a-conversation-with-anuk-arudpragasam/

program Mamoun had attended, met every day on Zoom. Rania shared a poem and Diane responded with a collage. In a conversation with Rania over Zoom, I asked her about how she experienced time during those early days of the pandemic, when the uprising was still roaring. She said 'I lived in Sudan's timezone, my attention fixed on the screen, unaware of anything else around me'. She said that at some point, the remoteness of exile and of the pandemic forced her back to herself. She describes *Something Evergreen* as 'not just a book but a journey of recovery'.

Rania wanders through an inner world, and carries back poems that are delicate, spare, and direct.

> last night
> the slender thread of light
> dancing in my darkened room
> lured me up
> I threw my boredom to the ground
> & like a lunatic i followed it
> to catch perhaps
> to hold in my cold palm
>
> (29 April 2020)

One poem is mainly made up of a single word:

> mourning
>
> (30 May 2020)

The poems sing in Yasmine Seale's translation:

> I live on the lip, split
> between slipping & holding

Seale bestows meticulous attention to carrying over not just the cadence of the Arabic, but its structure. It upends syntactical expectations in a way that lends the poems richness. The result is English that contains an Arabic quality.

> absence in nothing
> shrill whine in my head
>   on the news virus
>   deaths climb

Elsewhere, she writes:

> a fine spray
> of longing
> falls
> from a sky not a sky

Seale's many delightful choices—'riverskin' to float on top of, and time that 'mushrooms'—made me wish it had been a bilingual edition to admire her work more fully, line by line.

Something Evergreen exudes warmth and compassion. It conveys an interconnectedness despite the aches of violence, migration, and loss. It is a collection to read and reread.

> the gap is wide
> from here to there
>   but where is here
>   where there?

I'll start loving you from tomorrow

I'm your Poet: Selected Poems of Nilim Kumar (translated by
Dibyajyoti Sarma), Red River, 2022
Review by Amlanjyoti Goswami

Nilim Kumar is a poet of pithy certitudes. In essence a love poet, his
primary idiom is free verse, where vicissitudes of love are rendered in
a persuasive language of the everyday. This ability to write in an
intimate and familiar tone endears him to a ready audience, for whom
his poetry is solace, for love both lost and found. It also makes him a
popular presence in contemporary Assamese poetry.

Nilim Kumar's best work addresses concerns of love with a
compelling strangeness, perhaps also because such poetry is not
separate from the folk locales it comes from. His work is able to move
the reader as the poet transitions across changing emotional and
material landscapes. The resulting poetic tension is crackling.

As an example, consider this fragment of an estranged romantic's
oeuvre, for whom nature is both respite and sublimation:

In 'The Garden of Sleep', the poet writes:

> The oranges
> bathe in rain.
> Whimpering,
> the oranges get drenched.
> Nobody approaches
> the oranges.
> There is no shadow
> in rain.

Predictably, the poet's endeavours of the heart are not confined to nature alone. There are human beings too, living and dead. 'At the Dinner Table', he fondly recalls his mother, long gone.

> I was now older than my mother. Seeing me
> grown old, there were tears in her eyes.

Yet, this too is not enough. The poet wants to break free of all confines. He wants to trespass and enter other people's lives, where love perhaps resides.

In 'Tether', the poet confesses:

> I tether my heart
> otherwise, it eats flowers
> breaks fences
> intrudes into other's courtyard.

Apart from this, what is left in the verse is only the idea of love, nulled into a fine abstraction. There is hardly time for real love these days. The vicissitudes of daily life have taken over. In 'I'll start loving you from tomorrow', he addresses love in a businesslike manner:

> I'll start loving you from tomorrow,
> today I'm extremely busy.

In such light, the poet's more recent work is becoming predictable and monotonous. One misses the ironies of old. The modern city, always on the move, is disenchanted, and no longer interested in poetry or love. The poet is confined to the self, unable to break free or venture out, despite his wishes. There is an intimate tone, but one wonders to whom it is addressed. Are his poems becoming diary entries?

See for example, 'Save Poetry/Save the Mice', where the poet's concerns turn curiously orthopedic:

> It's been 21 days since I broke
> the heel of my left leg.
> As advised
> the leg now rests inside a white cast....

Or when, in 'Letters Arrive Frequently', he acknowledges the reality of a postal address:

> I get mails frequently
> at the address in the city
> where I don't reside,
> where my mail arrives.

Further, the task of detailing every aspect of experience into English is arduous, and sometimes falls short of conveying the essence of the poem, especially in some of the longer pieces. In 'Memoir', he laments his soul, wherever it exists:

> And my soul, immersed in its self, absorbed in
> the limitless horizon, which experiences its body,
> did not have the crook on its waist, neither were
> the poke marks on the body...

Later in the same poem, he bemoans that:

> those heartbreaking partings
> And goodbyes were my own, which I drank and on
> My heart grew an ocean of blue stone. It was not your
> Creation, O God. And Devil, wasn't I searched for
> The roots of those liquid trees?

It is difficult to render such emotion into English without mixing up meanings and metaphors. Transliterating theological abstractions such as the soul do not map easily onto the cultural contexts where the poet lives. The demon and the devil are not one in all cultures. Wherever the poet veers towards the ordinary while missing the enchantments of old, his lines are in danger of turning prosaic. He is troubled by modernity, but he lives in it. His rewards as a poet of repute are tied to being an intrinsic part of a modern universe—of the written word, publication and circulation. Yet he grapples with the coarseness of everyday life, filled as it is with betrayals and unpleasant surprises, where life always comes up short.

In 'Good Man', he realises the ethical cause of his suffering:

> I suffer whenever I meet a good man
> Because his sadness is limitless. Whenever we meet,
> I hug a good man and try to ascertain how deep
> He will sink, how deep.

This is a perennial dilemma of intent versus text that confronts every translator. Yet Dibyajyoti comes out somewhat unscathed from the encounter. Where he struggles is where the poet also struggles—in the intimate rendering of everyday detail in modern living, within the larger body of romantic love that the poet finds comfort in. It appears there is a tension in these poems between romanticism and modernity itself, which the poet is unable to reconcile. This needs to be situated in an urbanising Assam, where old villages and the familiar haunts of childhood give way to an unfamiliar, adult city.

Dibyajyoti Sarma's mission of translating Nilim Kumar's *Selected Poems* assumes critical significance. This is an ambitious and sincere effort from the translator, who is also a poet and publisher of a small press, Red River. Overall, the translator shows meticulous attention to detail and relentless persistence. This is the strength of the translation. Dibyajyoti is at his best when translating pithy lines, where meaning is conveyed in short bursts of epiphany. In 'Two Stones', both the translator and the poet evoke magic:

> she arrives
> from behind the hill
> we meet
> next to the lake
> neither of us speak—
> two stones.

This work will hopefully inspire more translations of other contemporary Assamese poets, such as Lutfa Halum Salima Begum, Sameer Tanti and Anubhav Tulasi, who deserve to be known outside Assam. Assamese poetry is vibrant, but publishing remains a difficult enterprise. Nilim Kumar's book of selected poems in Assamese, published in 2015, is already out of print and not available in bookstores. This translation by Red River may prod Banalata, his original publishers, to redress the situation, perhaps with a reprint. The market's vagaries are nothing new, but poetry continues to somehow thrive.

Locating a Polyphonous Bangla

Modern Bengali Poetry: Desire for Fire (selected and translated by
Arunava Sinha), Parthian Books, 2020
Review by Adrija Ghosh

Modern Bengali Poetry: Desire for Fire is an anthology archiving the
changing chronotropes of Bengali literary scenes in India, Bangladesh,
and overseas. Selected and translated by award-winning Indian
translator Arunava Sinha, this volume presents over fifty practitioners
of 'modern' Bengali poetry, across a span of a hundred years, to map
the desire for 'fire'—representing an energy that seeks change, not
only in the societies the poems address, but also in the form, style,
and lexicon that the poems are presented in.

The poets have been arranged chronologically to explore
the evolution of modern poetry to its current, contemporary
counterparts. It begins with Rabindranath Tagore, harbinger of
modernity in Bengali literature. The poems 'Camelia' and 'An
Unexpected Meeting' are testament to Tagore's control over the
language, his economy, as well as his cleverness of playing with
homophony and symbols of 'modernism' in colonised India, such as
the railways. However, he has also been seen as the tradition that poets
succeeding him must dismantle, the shadow they must overcome.

Many of the poets mentioned in this volume were born in an
erstwhile, undivided Bengal, as evident in the works of poets such as
Jibanananda Das, who chronicled the haunting despair of the 1947
Partition that split apart the Bengali community. From the urban
melancholy of Jibanananda Das, this volume travels to the poets of
the Kallol Jug (New Wave Poets); to the poet who discovered Das,
Buddhadeva Bose; to socialist poets such as Samar Sen, Subhash
Mukhopadhyay, and Marxist poet Sukanta Bhattacharya, known as

Kishor Kobi (or the Young Bard), who died at 21 years of age, and was a fierce critic of capitalism. His part-allegory, part-fable 'The Cock's Tale' notes that when the bird enters the mansion in search of food:

> Then one day he indeed got entry
> Managing to go directly
> To the banquet table draped in spotless linen;
> Not to have food, though—
> But as food.

This poem showcases his mature choice of form to articulate a lesson in class consciousness, and is in a similar vein to Manik Bandopadhyay, another Marxist, who wrote fierce anti-imperial protest poems such as 'Tea', where he observes:

> We bribe London to drink our tea
>
> The gardens are on our mountain slopes
> Our workers plant the seeds
> It's our labourers who pick the leaves
> They're naked, uncivilised, black-skinned.
> As black as burnt charcoal.
> Drinking the tea he makes, the white king says,
> What a perfect cup of tea.

The onslaught of famines in Bengal gave rise to the Food Movement in the late '50s, and consequently, the Bengali poetry scene saw the emergence of disillusioned young poets who wrote about extreme poverty, greed, corruption, and hunger of all sorts. Poems in this anthology by the likes of Subho Acharjya and Malay Roy Choudhury show how with a combination of anti-establishment rhetoric, bohemian values, and Freudian evocations, the self-proclaimed Hungryalists managed to rip apart the 'bhadralok' (the genteel class) sensibilities of Bengali readers. Shakti Chattopadhyay, although initially a part of the Hungryalists, changed his poetic voice towards a more anthropocentric one; the poem 'The Rain on Calcutta's Breast' expresses a complex urban ennui, almost a dreamlike state of being nostalgic about the present moment, a somewhat surreal nature being a quirk of the Krittibas School of Poets to which, along with Sunil Gangopadhyay, he belonged.

Bengali poetry during the '70s was mostly influenced by the Naxal Movement as well as the Liberation War. The anthology includes the explicit political poetic voices of Mallika Sengupta, Sankha Ghosh, and Nabarun Bhattacharya, as well as contemporary poets such as Joy Goswami and Srijato, who are comparatively less political. This expansive range of style, theme, and form lends a choral quality to the volume. The presence of feminist, anti-caste voices such as Kalyani Thakur Charal is a potent call to question the 'modern' canon of poetics and how it is being revised through revolution as well as reevaluation.

The selection of Bangladeshi poets reflects on the mercurial landscape of a war-ravaged land. Poet Nirmalendu Goon writes in 'Firearm':

Only I, disobeying the commands of the Army, have turned
Into a tender rebel—I return home in full view, and yet I hold
A firearm as dangerous as the heart, I haven't turned it in

The poetry of Syed Shamsul Haq; Shaheed Quaderi, whose poetry was used for graffiti in the Liberation War; and Asha Naznin range from experimental, to political, to romantic echoes of the anxieties of a generation that experienced the Partition, the

Liberation War (Mukti Juddho), the Language Movement (Bhasha Andolan) and the subsequent independence of Bangladesh, as well as succeeding generations that remain haunted by violence, separation, and revolt.

Loss is inevitable in translation. English acts as a medium that neutralises differences in inflections and dialects within the different kinds of Bengali used, and erases cultural fault-lines. Bengali is polyphonic in nature—the way it is spoken not only pertains to accents, dialects, but also in how certain letters are pronounced—and often it is a signifier of a person's social position. The Bengali of Tagore is modern, but it is comparatively more pristine and refined than that of the Hungryalists, who made a deliberate attempt to insert colloquial idioms and lexicon to pave the way for the 'low-brow' in their literature, which is what made their works tabloid in nature.

The way Bengali is colloquially spoken is captured in 'অনাবশ্যক কবিতা' ('A redundant poem') by the Hungryalist Phalguni Roy. In the Bengali version, the poet ponders:

এখন কবরি হাতের শরির কেটে যখন রক্ত নিচ্ছেন চিকিৎসক
তখন আমার মনে পড়ছে আমি নিজের রক্ত বেচে মদ
গিলে লিখিতে চেয়েছিলুম কবিতা
আমি কি উচ্ছন্নে গেছি?

The deliberate attempt by the poet to sound informal, self-deprecating, and impertinent cannot be replicated in English—the poet is not simply talking about drinking alcohol here; when consuming is referred to with the word 'গিলে', it is usually signaled to be crude and undignified. Thus, the solitary presence of the word 'গিলে' (transliteration: 'swallow'), at the beginning of the poem, aims to transform the poetic voice into an 'unsophisticated' one almost instantaneously. It sets the tone of the poem and acts as a signpost for the personality of the narrator.

In the translated text, it is replaced with 'to drink and write poetry', which undercuts the desperate undertone of the narrator, who was willing to bargain his blood for alcohol that would let him create. It is one of the many ways in which nuance disappears; the poem is defiant in its theme but loses the impertinence of language that would traditionally be considered 'low-brow', a deliberate aesthetic choice made by the Hungry generation to represent the masses.

Sinha calls himself a 'translator-performer' in the translator's overture, and he has managed to put up a show that highlights a range of Bengali 'modern' poetry across time, gender, class, caste, and borders. In a way, this anthology erases both literal and linguistic borders and boundaries. Poems that were written during the Liberation War resonated with those who were believers in the Naxalite ideology because of the shared timeline of events. Similarly, poets in both India and Bangladesh who were suddenly confronted with Western imports and privatisation, with the advent of neoliberal capitalism, wrote across borders about the same sense of growing alienation. This collection paves the way to expand our knowledge of the canon, and to pay close attention to the voices who were previously excluded from it.

NOTES ON CONTRIBUTORS

AARON AQUILINA is a resident academic with the Department of English at the University of Malta. He has published academic material but also writes poetry, short stories, and creative criticism.

ABID RAZA was born in Pakistan and lives in United States. A physician by profession, he has translated some contemporary Urdu poets and is currently working on an anthology.

ABIGAIL ARDELLE ZAMMIT is a Maltese writer whose English poetry has appeared in various British and American journals. Her main interests are place, feminist poetics and the body's consciousness.

ADRIAN GRIMA (1968) writes poetry and prose in Maltese for adults and children and has read his work at festivals in many countries. He teaches Maltese literature at the University of Malta and Maltese language at Inalco, Paris.

ADRIANA DÍAZ ENCISO is a Mexican poet, novelist and translator. Her latest publication is *Flint* (Contraband Books). She lives in London, where she's working on her fifth novel.

ADRIJA GHOSH is a queer, polyglot poet, translator, and filmmaker. Their debut collection of multilingual poetry, *the commerce between tongues* is forthcoming in June 2023 with Broken Sleep Books. @byadrija

ALBERT GATT has translated several works of poetry and prose, including works by Adrian Grima, Immanuel Mifsud, Walid Nabhan and Clare Azzopardi. He works at Utrecht University and the University of Malta.

ALFREDO ESPINO was born in Ahuachapán, El Salvador in 1900. His only book, *Jicaras Tristes*, a collection of 96 poems, was published posthumously following his suicide in 1928.

ALFRED PALMA, the translator, is best known for the complete and rhymed Maltese translation of Dante's *Divina Commedia* and that of great authors such as Shakespeare, Oscar Wilde, Voltaire, D.H. Lawrence and Thomas Mann.

AMLANJYOTI GOSWAMI's new poetry collection, *Vital Signs* (Poetrywala) follows his earlier book, *River Wedding* (Poetrywala). Published widely across the world, he grew up in Guwahati and lives in Delhi.

ANTOINE CASSAR is a London-born Maltese poet, translator and editor. He is the author of *Erbgħin Jum* (Forty Days, 2018 National Book Prize) and *Passaport*, a long poem adapted for the stage in seven countries.

AYA NABIH is a translator and writer born in Cairo. She is the author of the poetry collection *Exercises to Develop Insomnia Skills* (Al-Kotob Khan, 2015).

CHEN XIANFA (b.1967) is an Anhui-based Chinese poet, author of over a dozen poetry collections and two collections of essays. Awards include the Chen Zi'ang Poetry Prize (2016) and Lu Xun Literature Prize (2018).

CHETANA TIRTHAHALLI is the pen name of Gayathri HN (b. 1978). The author of four poetry collections, her interests include philosophy, cinema, spirituality, and the study of literature and culture.

CLARE AZZOPARDI is an award-winning writer who writes for both children and adults. Her work has been translated into several languages and has appeared in a number of collections including *Transcript*, *Cúirt 21*, *Words without Borders* and *Asymptote*.

CLAUDIA GAUCI lives in Malta and writes mainly poetry. She has published two collections of poetry and she is very much involved in the local literary scene. Gauci teaches Maltese literature at the Junior College, a post-secondary institution.

DAVID HUERTA (Mexico, 1949–2022) was one of Mexico's most beloved poets. Winner of many prestigious awards, he's remembered for his prolific work as poet and critic, his generosity, and his commitment to the teaching of poetry. He taught many how to read the world as a poet. As a columnist, he was distinguished by his lucidity and, when needed, fierce dissent. A truly irreplaceable figure in Latin American culture.

DYLAN CARPENTER teaches at the Catholic University of America and the University of Maryland.

GABRIEL ARAUJO (Venezuela) has translated the poetry of Marianne Moore, Derek Walcott and Verónica Jaffé, among others. He holds a PhD in Hispanic Studies from the University of London.

GIOELE GALEA has published two memoirs and seven collections of poetry, all of which give witness to an uncompromising spiritual journey, where bareness is as overwhelming as it is essential.

GLEN CALLEJA is a Maltese artist mainly interested in poetry and the book as object. His artistic work often involves alternative book structures, found content and performative elements.

HELENA CAMILLERI is reading for a master's degree in translation at the University of Heidelberg. She is passionate about language and literature, and dreams of combining the two in becoming a literary translator.

IMMANUEL MIFSUD lectures at the University of Malta. He is a five-time national literary award winner, a European Union Prize for Literature recipient, and the president of PEN Malta.

IRENE MANGION is a Maltese professional translator, mostly working between English, Maltese and French. Her translations of poetry, novels, plays and short stories have been published in France and Malta.

JASMINE BAJADA is a Gozitan poet. Her poetry has been published in *Mediterranean Poetry* and *Modern Poetry in Translation*. *wild tongue* is her upcoming debut poetry collection.

JESMOND SHARPLES, a nurse by profession, was Chief Nursing Officer for Malta (2002–2016). He writes poetry mostly in Maltese and English. He also studied Music Composition, Maltese Literature, Gerontology and Management. He has published two poetry books in Maltese, *Il-Qtar li Nħobb* (2016) and *Ra* (2019).

K SATCHIDANANDAN (b.1946) is a bilingual poet, critic, playwright, editor, fiction writer and travel writer. His latest books of poetry in English include *The Missing Rib*, *Not Only the Oceans* (Poetrywala,

Bombay) and *Singing in the Dark* (ed. with Nishi Chawla, Penguin-Random House, India). *Greening the Earth*, an international anthology of eco-poetry he edited, is due for publication from Penguin Random House.

KARINA FIORINI, a poet and an environmentalist (b. Malta), has a BA in Geography, a BA in English, a MSc in Sustainable Development. *Habiba*, her latest work, was highly commended by Joelle Taylor (Ledbury Poetry 2022). www.karinafiorini.com

KARL SCHEMBRI is a media adviser with Norwegian Refugee Council, covering frontlines of humanitarian crises in the Middle East and East Africa. Former journalist, author of novels, short stories, poetry and children's books.

KAT STORACE is a Maltese editor, translator and co-founder of Praspar Press. Her English translation of *what will it take for me to leave* by Loranne Vella was shortlisted for the Society of Authors TA First Translation Prize 2022.

LEANNE ELLUL writes poetry and prose. She has written about the sea, whiteness, and trees. In an ideal world, she will live in a tree house covered in snow, surrounded by sea.

LI HAI is a lecturer at Hefei University of Technology, also a PhD candidate at Hunan Normal University, who has published three books of translation (from English into Chinese), including Kitty Fitzgerald's *Pigtopia*.

LUKE GALEA is a poet and translator of poetry from Maltese/English into English/Maltese. He holds a MA in English Studies and a PhD in Phonetics.

M P PRATHEESH is the author of several collections of poetry and essays in Malayalam. He was awarded the Kedarnath Singh Memorial Poetry Prize in 2022. His recent publications include *Transfiguring Places* (Paper View, Portugal) and *The Burial* (forthcoming, Osmosis Press, UK). He lives and works in Kerala, India.

MADHAV AJJAMPUR is a writer and translator. His essays, poems, and translations have appeared in several Indian and international publications. His first book, *The Pollen Waits On Tiptoe*, was published in 2022.

MARIA GRECH GANADO (1943) translates from Maltese into English. Her poetry has been translated into 14 languages and has won four National Book Prizes. In 2005, she co-organised an international seminar in Malta.

MARIE GION is a Maltese poet, author and playwright. *Għax id-Drogi Sbieħ* (self-published, 2013) is her first collection of poetry. She was awarded a PhD in 2018, after which she went on to study the pianoforte. She is currently working on various literary projects.

MAYADA IBRAHIM is a New York-based translator, editor and writer, working in Arabic and English. Her translations have been published by Africa Institute (UAE), *Circumference Magazine* (US), Archipelago Books (US), Banipal (UK), and Willows House (South Sudan). She participated as a judge in PEN America's Literary Translation Prize 2021.

MEENA KANDASAMY is a poet, novelist and translator. Her books of poetry include *Touch* and *Ms Militancy*, and she is the author of three acclaimed novels, *Gypsy Goddess*, *When I Hit You* and *Exquisite Cadavers*.

MIRIAM CALLEJA is a poet, fiction/nonfiction writer, and translator. She has published poetry collections, collaborations, and chapbooks. Her work has appeared in journals and in translation worldwide.

MOHAMMAD-ALI SEPANLOU is an Iranian poet and literary critic. Nicknamed the Poet of Tehran, Sepanlou was also a founding member of the Writers' Association of Iran. Among other accolades, he was the recipient of *Légion d'honneur* and *Le prix Max-Jacob* for his literary and scholarly achievements. Sepanlou died in May 2015, aged 74.

NADIA MIFSUD is the author of three books of poetry, one chapbook, one novel and one collection of short stories. She is currently Malta's Poet Laureate.

NANCY NAOMI CARLSON won the 2022 Oxford-Weidenfeld Translation Prize and is the Translations Editor for *On the Seawall*. Her most recent co-translation was recommended by *The New York Times*.

NORBERT BUGEJA is one of Malta's foremost contemporary poets. He is Associate Professor within the Department of English and Director of the Mediterranean Institute at the University of Malta.

OMAR SEGUNA, the poet, has published three books: *Mal-Ħoss Qawwi tar-ragħad* (2001), *24, Triq Ħad-Dwieli* (2011) and *Xehir fis-skiet* (2019). Some of his writings have appeared in several anthologies.

PRISCILLA CASSAR is a therapist, geragogist and a poet, interested in arts-in-health. Her poetry, prose and translations have been published in a number of anthologies and projects, locally, online, as well as abroad. She continues working on her first collection of poems.

RAFIQ SANDEELVI is well known to the world of Urdu poetry. Born in 1961, he teaches literature in Pakistan. He has been published frequently in journals and has several collections.

RITA SALIBA's favourite genre is microfiction. She's published seven collections of short stories. Other publications include three teen novels and an adult novel, before publishing her recent book of verse.

RUTH WARD's creative collaborations center on the Mediterranean, particularly Malta and Spain. A member of PEN America, her literary translations have been published in English-speaking communities across the world.

SAMIRA NEGROUCHE is a prize-winning poet and translator born in Algiers, where she continues to live and work. Author of many poetry collections and artists' books, she enjoys engaging in multidisciplinary collaborations.

SANA GOYAL is Deputy and Reviews Editor at Wasafiri magazine. Her writing has appeared in *The Guardian*, *Poetry London*, *TLS*, and elsewhere. She lives between Birmingham and Bombay.

SARA ELKAMEL is a poet, journalist and translator based in Cairo. She is the author of the chapbook *Field of No Justice* (African Poetry Book Fund & Akashic Books, 2021).

SIAVASH SAADLOU is a writer and literary translator whose short stories and essays have been nominated for the Pushcart Prize and Best of the Net. His poetry has been anthologized in *Odes to Our Undoing* (Risk Press) and *Essential Voices: Poetry of Iran and Its Diaspora* (Green Linden Press). Saadlou is the winner of the 55th Cole Swensen Prize for Translation.

VERÓNICA JAFFÉ (Caracas, Venezuela) has published essays on Venezuelan literature, several poetry books and translations, and exhibited her visual poems. She has also taught in her home country and been editor of several literary magazines.